BODY SYSTEMS

THE DIGESTIVE SYSTEM

BY GOLRIZ GOLKAR

CONTENT CONSULTANT
ANTHONY J. WEINHAUS, PhD
ASSISTANT PROFESSOR
DEPARTMENT OF INTEGRATIVE BIOLOGY & PHYSIOLOGY
DIRECTOR, PROGRAM IN HUMAN ANATOMY
UNIVERSITY OF MINNESOTA

Kids Core

An Imprint of Abdo Publishing
abdobooks.com

abdobooks.com

Printed in the United States of America, North Mankato, Minnesota.
102022
012023

THIS BOOK CONTAINS
RECYCLED MATERIALS

Cover Photos: Shusha Guna/Shutterstock Images, body; Elena Kazanskaya/Shutterstock Images, intestine; Shutterstock Images, mouth; Andy Frith/Shutterstock Images, background
Interior Photos: Prostock Studio/Shutterstock Images, 4–5; Shutterstock Images, 6, 15, 16, 18–19, 28, 29; Monkey Business Images/iStockphoto, 8; Monkey Business Images/Shutterstock Images, 10–11, 12; Biophoto Associates/Science Source, 13; Steve Gschmeissner/Science Source, 21; Dr. Cecil H. Fox/Science Source, 22; Pixologic Studio/Science Source, 25; Elena Veselova/Shutterstock Images, 26

Editor: Ann Schwab
Series Designer: Ryan Gale

Library of Congress Control Number: 2021952328

Publisher's Cataloging-in-Publication Data

Names: Golkar, Golriz, author.
Title: The digestive system / by Golriz Golkar
Description: Minneapolis, Minnesota : Abdo Publishing, 2023 | Series: Body systems | Includes online resources and index.
Identifiers: ISBN 9781532198571 (lib. bdg.) | ISBN 9781098272227 (ebook)
Subjects: LCSH: Digestive organs--Juvenile literature. | Digestive system--Juvenile literature. | Digestion--Juvenile literature. | Gastrointestinal system--Juvenile literature. | Human anatomy--Juvenile literature.
Classification: DDC 612.3--dc23

CONTENTS

Everything a person eats or drinks enters the body through the digestive system.

CHAPTER 1

WHAT IS THE DIGESTIVE SYSTEM?

Melissa is excited about her lunch. First, she enjoys a ham and cheese sandwich. She chews every bite carefully before swallowing. Then Melissa munches on apple slices. The sweet flavor makes her mouth water.

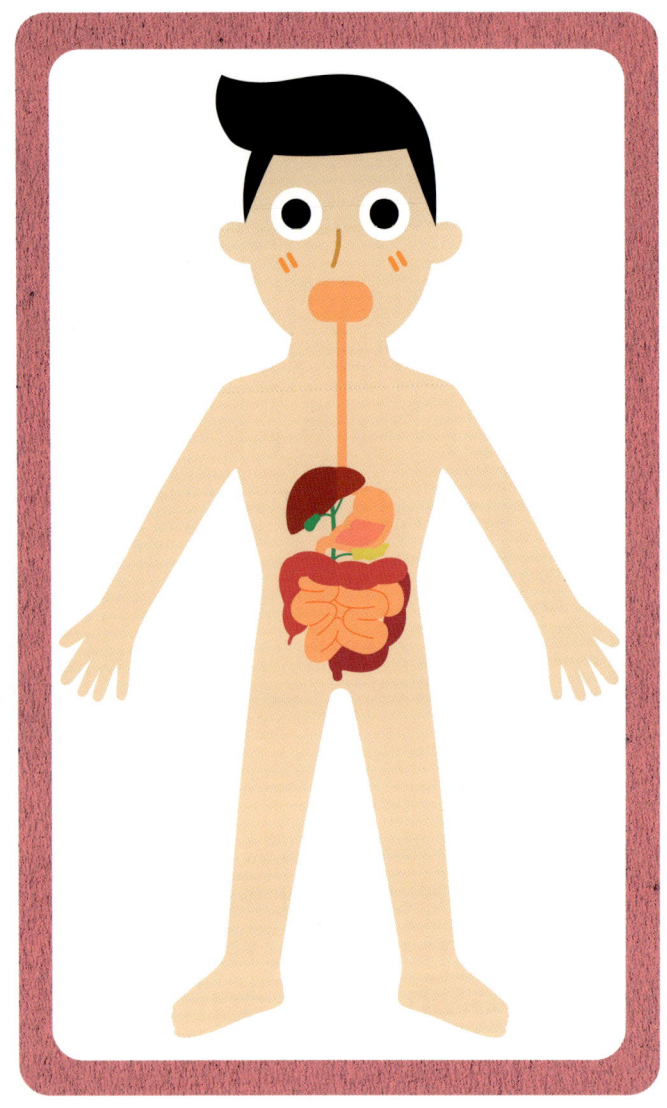

After a meal, food is broken down by the digestive system. Then the nutrients from the food are used by the entire body.

She nibbles on a cookie and drinks some milk. Now she feels full. It's play time! Melissa forgets all about her lunch. Her body, however, has important work to do. It needs to digest her lunch. This process converts food into fuel for her body. This will allow her body to function properly.

A Multistep Process

Digesting food takes many steps. Chewing and digestive juices help break down food particles. The body then **absorbs** the **nutrients** from the food and liquids. This process takes about eight hours.

Digest Quickly, Digest Slowly

The body does not digest all nutrients at the same rate. Carbohydrates are digested the fastest. They include starches and sugars. Proteins and fats take longer. That's why foods that contain protein and fat are more filling than other foods.

The digestive system converts the food people eat
into the fuel they need to live.

Nutrients include proteins, fats, carbohydrates, vitamins, and minerals. They give people energy. They help people grow. Nutrients also fix damaged cells. The digestive system helps people stay healthy. Just as a car uses gasoline to run, the body uses nutrients to function. The digestive system makes sure the body has fuel to keep it going.

Further Evidence

Look at the website below. Does it give any new evidence to support Chapter One?

Your Digestive System

abdocorelibrary.com/digestive-system

The sight and smell of food begin the digestion process.

CHAPTER 2

HOW DIGESTION BEGINS

Digestion begins before the first bite. When a person sees or smells food, glands in the mouth release saliva. Most people make about 5 cups (1.2 L) of saliva every day.

Teeth cut and grind food into small bits that mix with saliva to be swallowed.

Saliva contains chemicals called enzymes. Enzymes break down food. They turn it into simpler substances that the body can absorb. As a person chews, the teeth cut food into

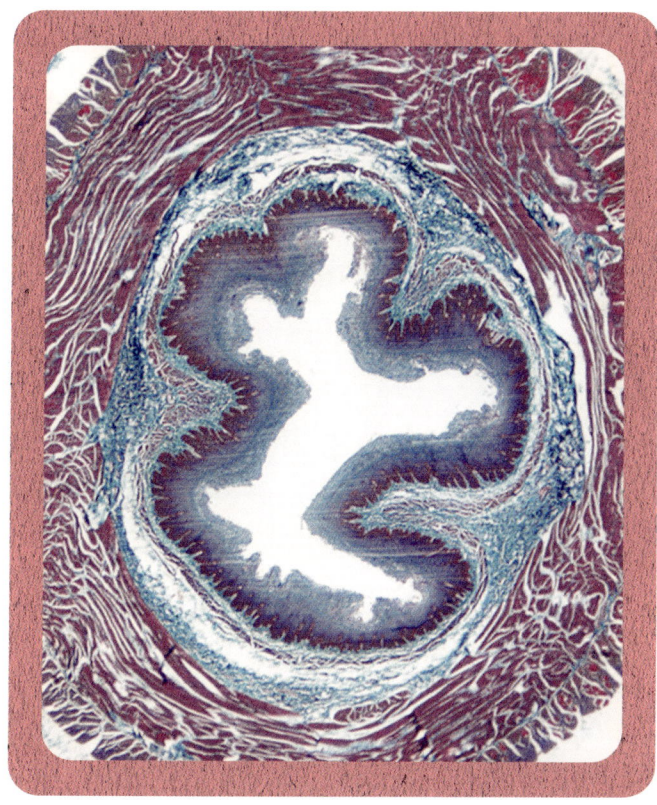

A magnified cross-section of the esophagus, as seen under a microscope

smaller pieces. The tongue helps move it around. Saliva moistens the food. This makes the food easier to swallow.

Going Down

The tongue pushes food down the throat. The food travels down a tube called the esophagus.

A small tissue flap, the epiglottis, closes over the nearby windpipe, called the trachea.

The trachea carries air to the lungs and is used for breathing. The epiglottis keeps food out of the trachea.

Going Down the Wrong Way

Sometimes, food and liquids go down the trachea by mistake. The epiglottis may not have enough time to cover the trachea. A person may cough or choke. This can be avoided by eating slowly, without talking.

Going Down the Right Pipe

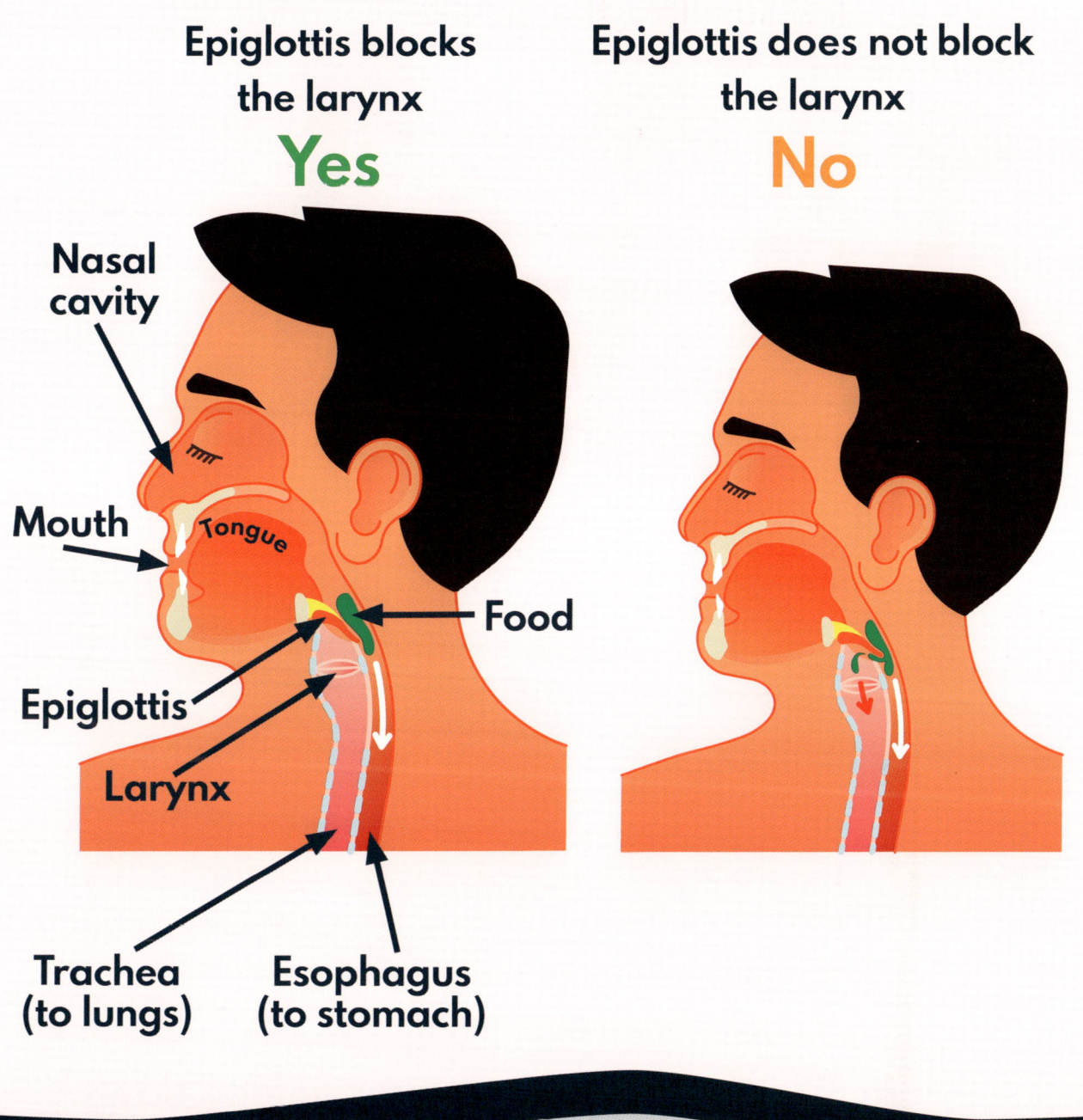

Epiglottis blocks
the larynx
Yes

Epiglottis does not block
the larynx
No

Nasal
cavity

Mouth

Tongue

Food

Epiglottis

Larynx

Trachea
(to lungs)

Esophagus
(to stomach)

When food is swallowed, the epiglottis blocks the entrance to the trachea. This allows the food to go down the esophagus to the stomach. It also helps prevent choking.

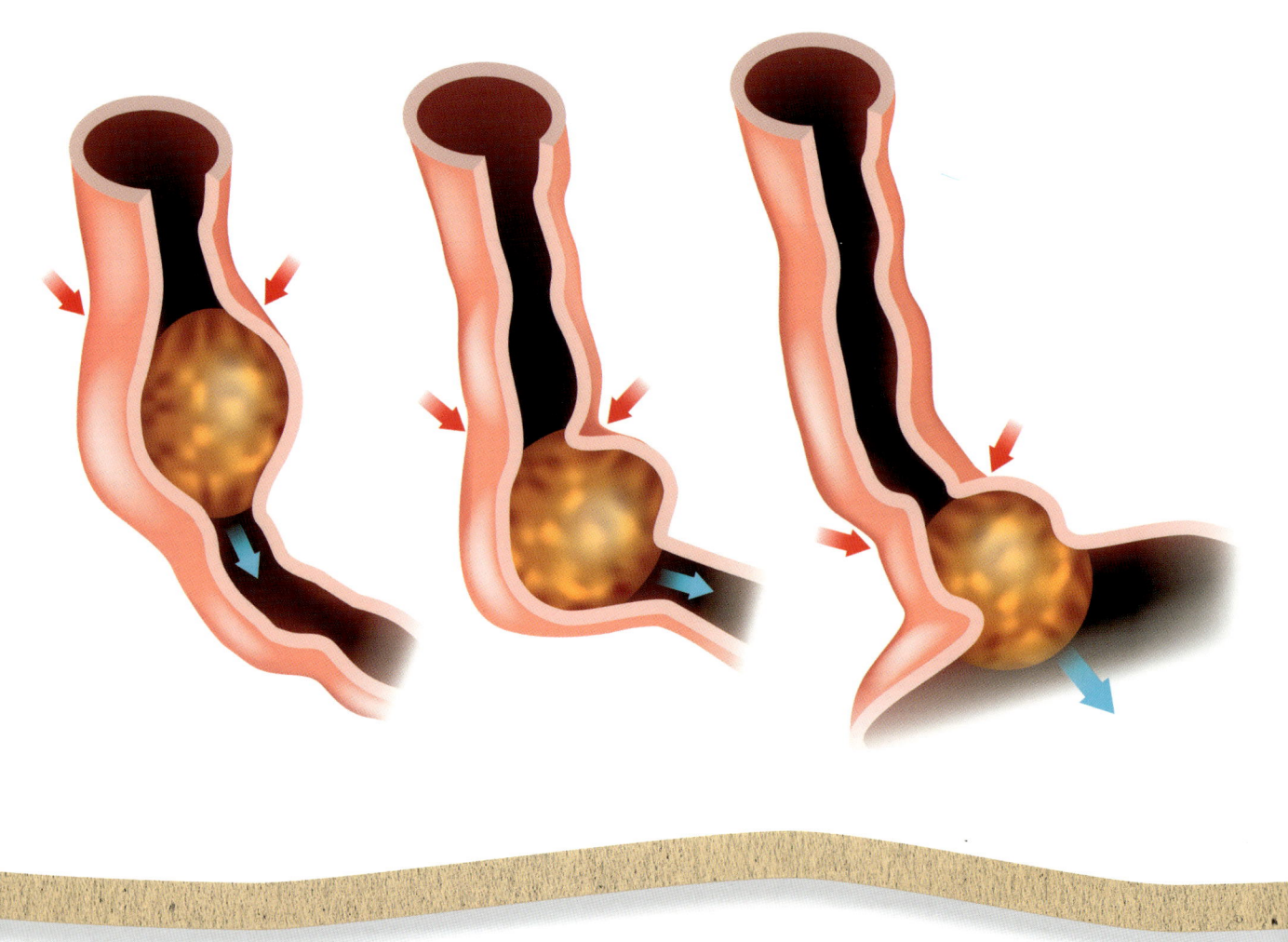

The strong muscle movement of the esophagus pushing food to the stomach is called peristalsis.

Muscles in the esophagus move food down the tube. These muscle movements are very strong. They can push food down the tube even if a person is upside down! They help make sure food goes to the stomach.

Finally, food reaches the end of the esophagus. A ringlike muscle relaxes to let it pass into the stomach. When a person is not eating, this muscle usually stays closed. This prevents the food in the stomach from going back up the esophagus.

Explore Online

Visit the website below. Does it give any new information about the digestive system that wasn't in Chapter Two?

How Do You Digest Food?

abdocorelibrary.com/digestive-system

The stomach's digestive juices help digest both foods and liquids, like milk.

CHAPTER 3

FUELING THE BODY

In the stomach, food is digested even more. Stomach muscles mix food with enzymes and **acids**. These digestive juices are produced by cells lining the stomach wall. They produce more than 8 cups (1.9 L) of strong acid every day.

The digestive juices break down nutrients and kill bad **bacteria**. The food turns into a thick mixture called chyme. When the nutrients are fully digested, the chyme is slowly released into the small intestine. This is a long, muscular tube that is bunched up in coils. In adults, it is about 22 feet (6.7 m) long. Within it, digestive juices break down the chyme.

Two large glands, the pancreas and liver, help the small intestine. The pancreas sends enzymes. They break down the chyme into proteins, fats, and carbohydrates. The liver sends a fluid called bile. It breaks down fats and helps the body absorb vitamins.

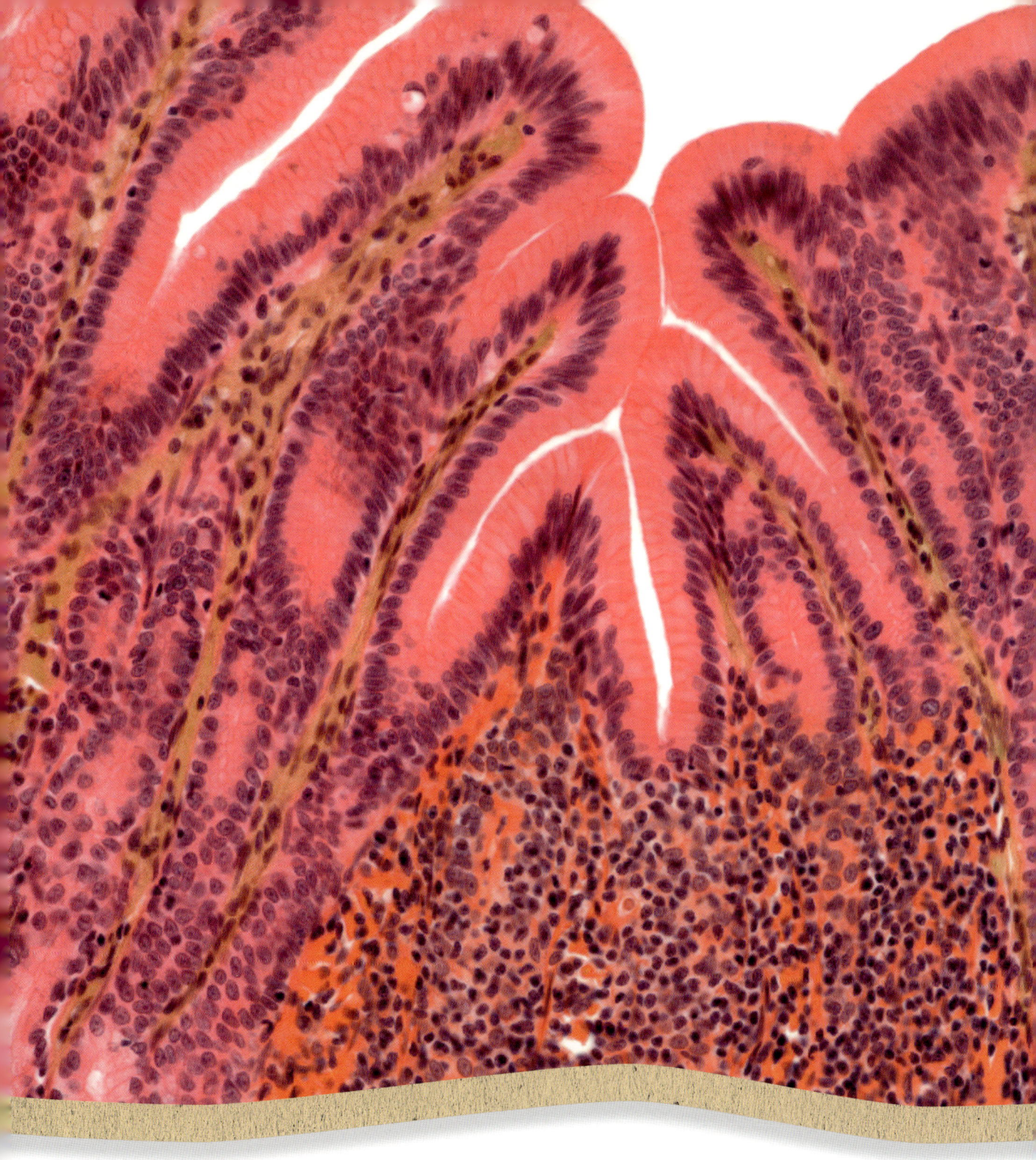

The stomach lining, shown here magnified by a microscope, creates mucus. This sticky substance protects the lining from stomach acid.

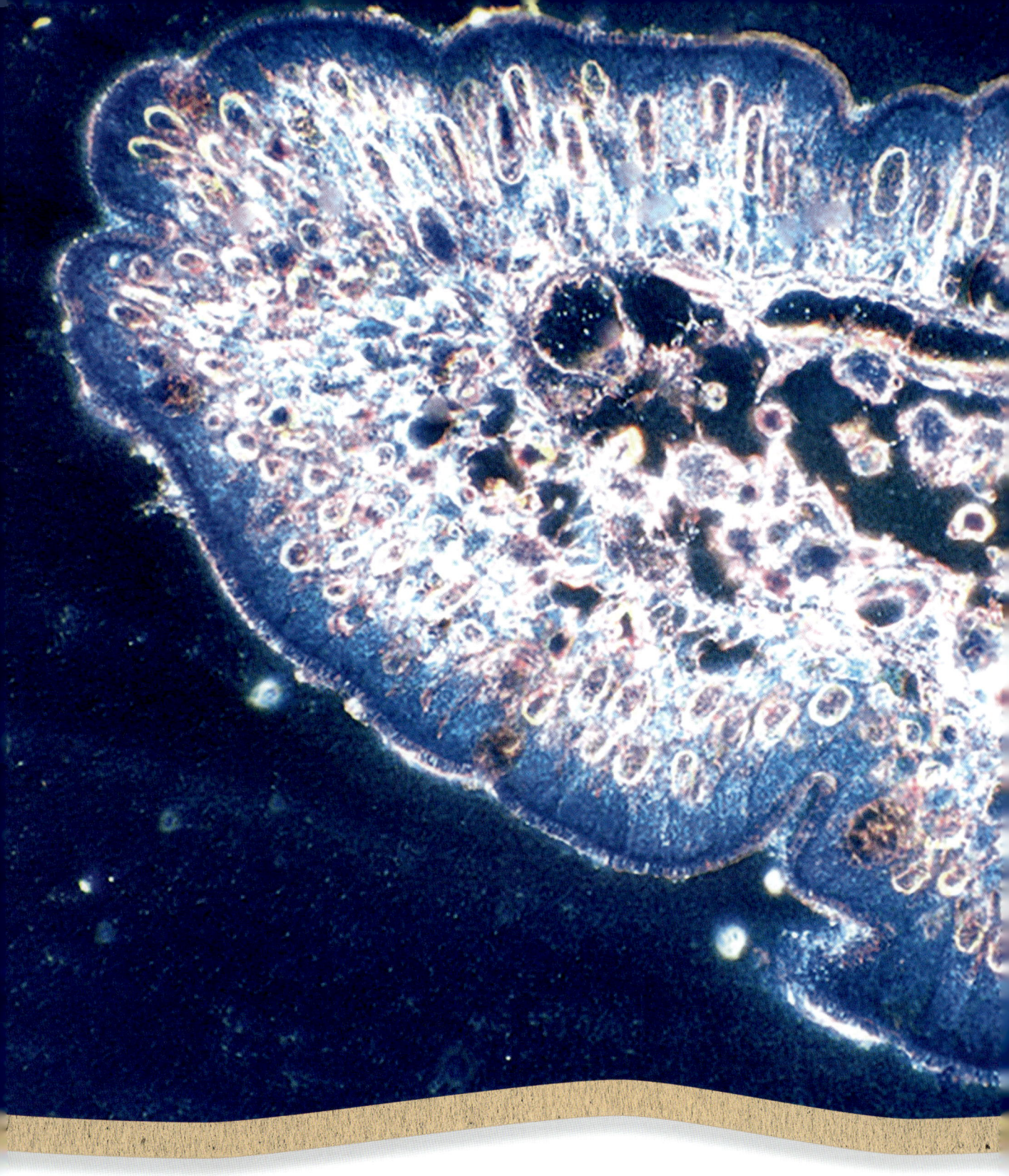

Millions of villi line the small intestine. The one shown here is magnified 800 times its actual size.

Entering the Bloodstream

The intestinal walls are lined with millions of villi. They are tiny, fingerlike folds. As the chyme travels through the small intestine, nutrients are absorbed by the villi. They transport the nutrients into the bloodstream. The nutrient-rich blood is carried to the liver. The liver removes any **toxic** substances. These substances later exit the body as waste.

The liver sends nutrient-rich blood to the heart through the bloodstream. This blood then flows to the lungs. The lungs provide the blood with oxygen. The bloodstream carries nutrients and oxygen to every cell in the body.

After the body has absorbed nutrients, some food will still be undigested. This waste passes through the large intestine. This tube is about 5 feet (1.5 m) long. Here, water is removed and absorbed into the bloodstream. The body cannot use what is left after that. It removes the waste as stool.

The Brain's Role in Digestion

Nerves and chemical messengers called hormones send signals to the brain. These signals help the brain manage digestion. Together, they control muscles and the production of digestive juices. They also tell us when we feel hungry or full.

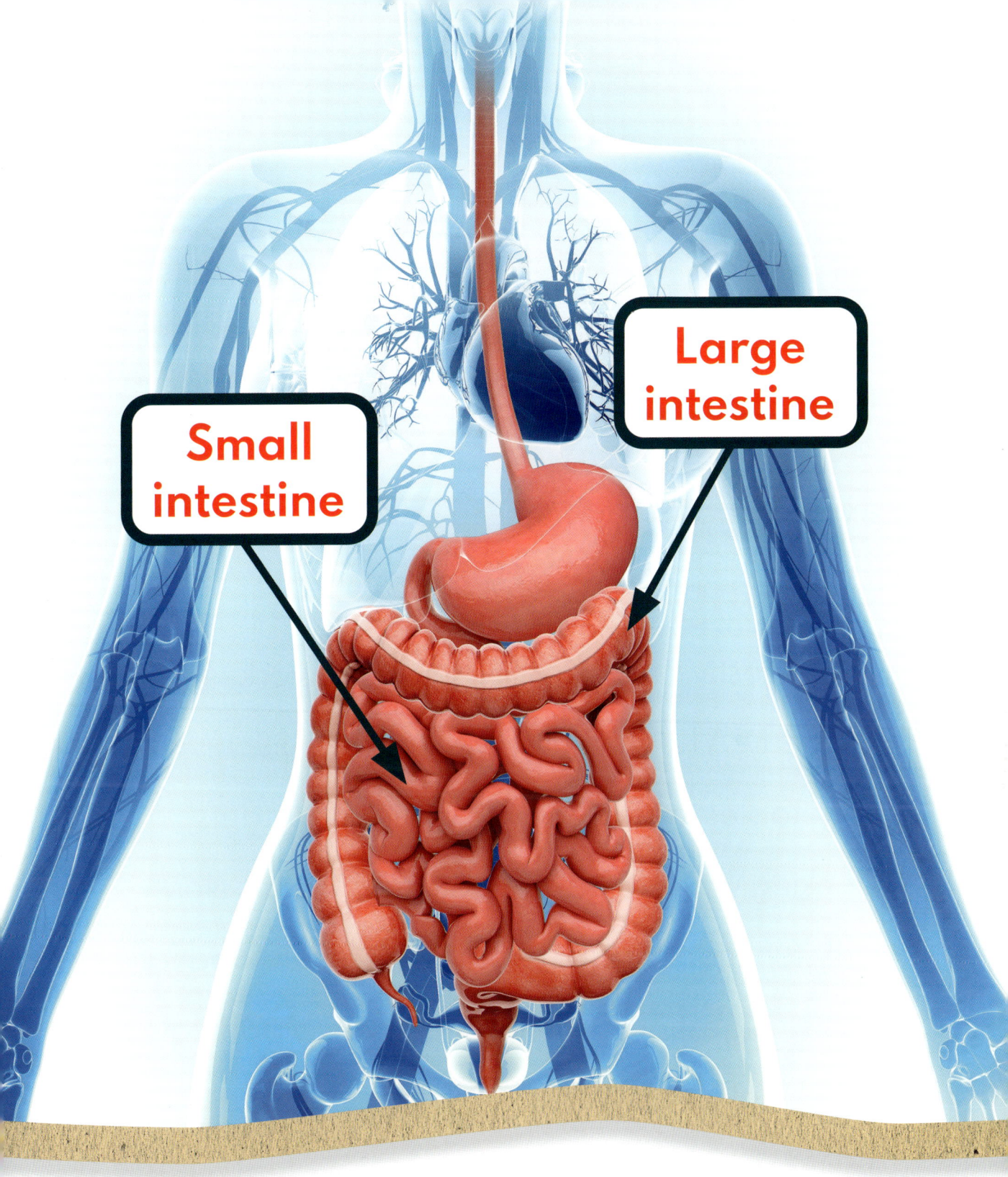

Small intestine

Large intestine

The large intestine sits below the stomach and frames the small intestine.

It's helpful to eat foods rich in good bacteria, such as yogurt. Good bacteria aid in digestion.

Helping Digestion

The digestive system needs care to work properly. A healthy diet with lots of fruits, vegetables, and whole grains is important. Drinking water is also important. Water helps cells function. It also helps break down food for easier digestion. Exercise increases blood flow, which helps the digestive system work well. Taking good care of the digestive system helps the whole body stay healthy.

Dr. Vincent Ho studies the digestive system. He explains how bile helps digestion:

> Bile is a yellow-green, thick, sticky juice that acts like washing powder. It helps break big chunks of fat from oily foods into little pieces.

Source: Vincent Ho, "Curious Kids: How Does My Tummy Turn Food into Poo?" *The Conversation*, 25 Feb. 2019, theconversation.com. Accessed 15 Nov. 2021.

What's the Big Idea?

Read this quote carefully. What is its main idea? Explain how the main idea is supported by details.

SYSTEM MAP

Fold of lining in small intestine

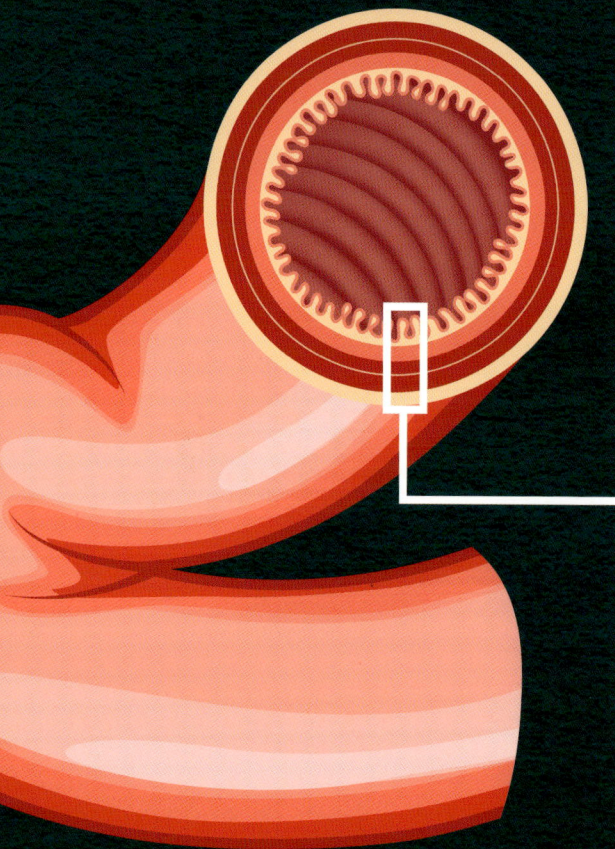

Small intestine

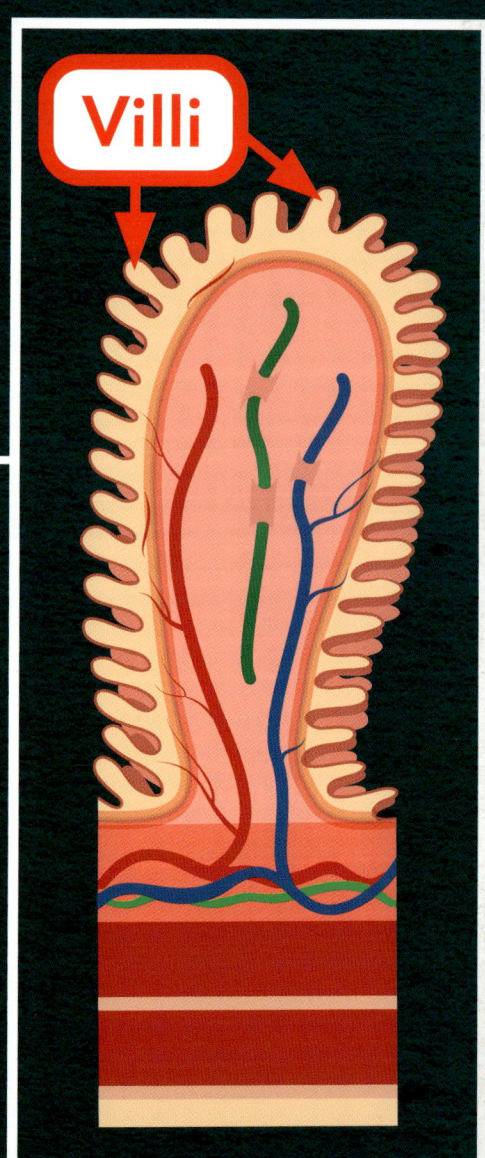

Villi

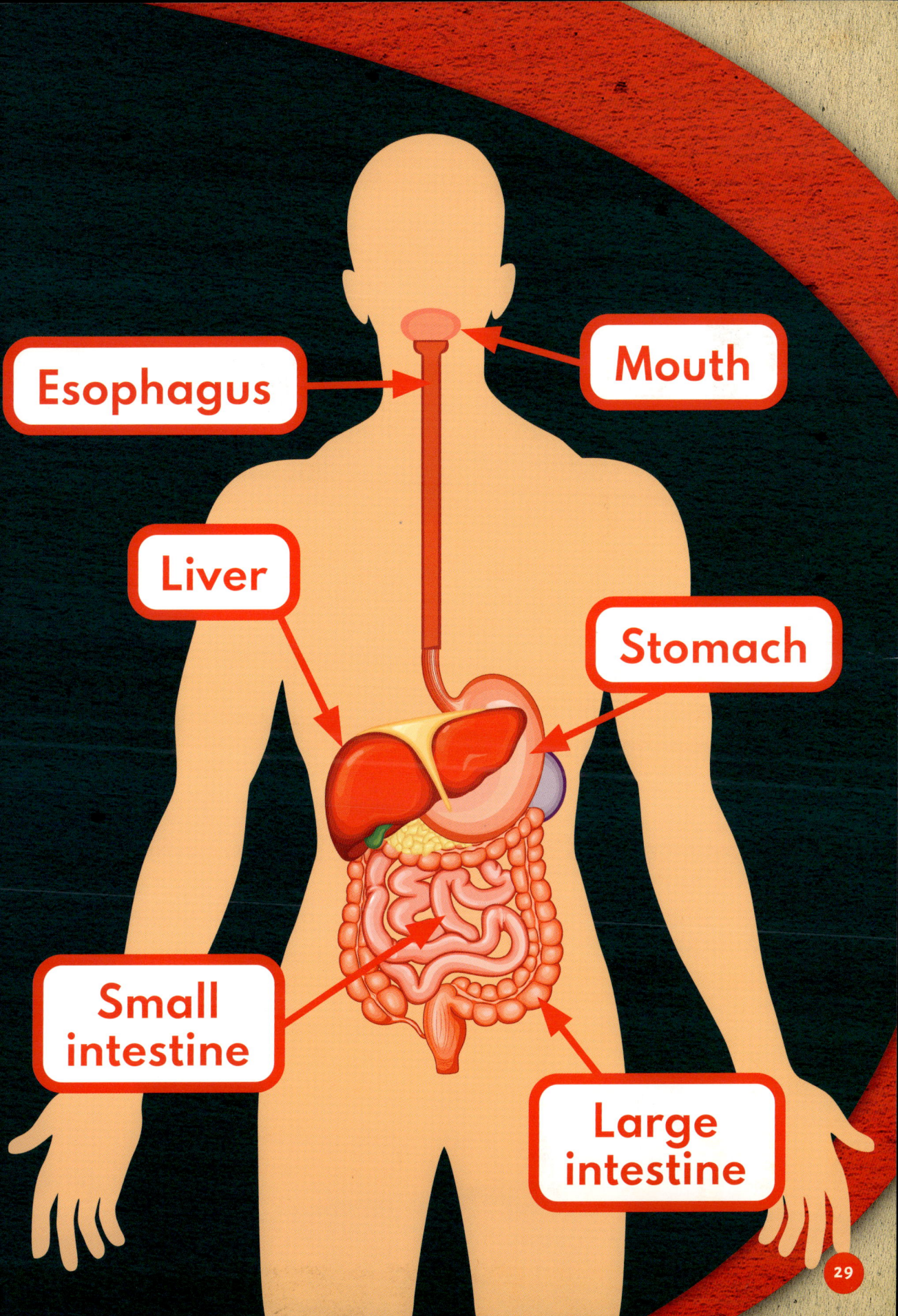

Esophagus

Mouth

Liver

Stomach

Small intestine

Large intestine

29

Glossary

absorbs
takes in or soaks up

acid
a chemical fluid with a sour taste that can dissolve other substances; stomach acid helps to digest food

bacteria
very small, single-celled organisms found in all natural environments

cell
the smallest and most basic unit of life; tissues and organs are formed from cells

nutrients
substances used by an organism to survive and grow

toxic
poisonous or harmful to one's health

Online Resources

To learn more about the digestive system, visit our free resource websites below.

Visit **abdocorelibrary.com** or scan this QR code for free Common Core resources for teachers and students, including vetted activities, multimedia, and booklinks, for deeper subject comprehension.

Visit **abdobooklinks.com** or scan this QR code for free additional online weblinks for further learning. These links are routinely monitored and updated to provide the most current information available.

Learn More

Troup, Roxanne. *The Circulatory System*. Abdo, 2023.

Wagner, Kristie. *Human Anatomy for Kids*. Rockridge, 2021.

Index

About the Author

Golriz Golkar is a former elementary school teacher. She has written more than 50 nonfiction books for children. She loves to sing and spend time with her young daughter.